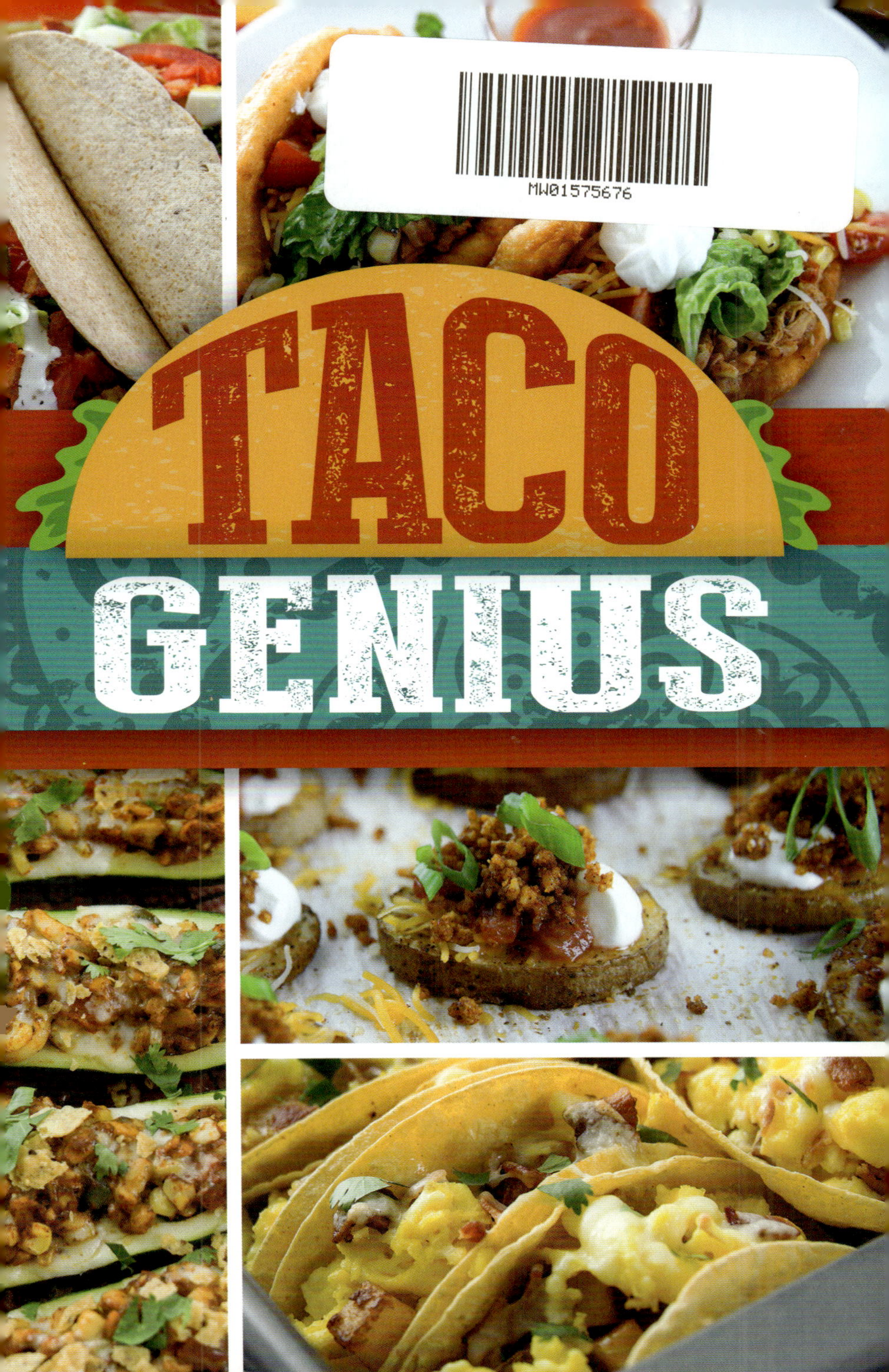
MW01575676
TACO
GENIUS

Hot Taco Tips

- ◆ When cutting up jalapeños or other hot peppers, wear gloves to protect your hands from the burning oils they contain.

- ◆ Use caution when frying shells in hot oil and never leave the stove, pans, or deep-fryer unattended. A deep-frying thermometer will help maintain the right temperature.

- ◆ Feel free to adjust spiciness levels to your personal taste – start with less seasoning if you like milder dishes, add more if you like things hot.

Printed in the United States of America
by G&R Publishing Co.

Distributed By:

507 Industrial Street
Waverly, IA 50677

ISBN-13: 978-1-56383-397-7
Item #7130

Tacos Unleashed

Who says a taco has to have meat and cheese? Unleash exciting new flavors you never dreamed of putting inside a crisp shell or soft roll-up. Or skip traditional shells altogether and stuff delicious fillings into something entirely different – think pasta shells, scooped-out veggies, wontons, or even cinnamon rolls.

Shell Games

◆ Choose your size – flour and corn tortillas are available in 6″, 8″, or 10″ varieties. *(Bigger ones are easier for rolls and wraps.)*

◆ If you like soft shells, just heat tortillas in a microwave or dry skillet until they're nice and flexible, or wrap them in foil for oven or grill warming.

◆ Like 'em crispy instead? No problem. Simply buy them that way – or turn soft tortillas crisp when you bake, broil, grill, or fry them. *(Check out the fun tricks on page 62.)*

◆ Try your hand at homemade tortillas or fry up refrigerated doughs for puff-tastic flavor and crunch.

◆ Mix and match your fillings and shells for even more taco-rific fun. It's your game so play it your way!

For appetizers, meals, and desserts, this is Taco Genius!

Sweet Potato Breakfast Tacos

1 (20 oz.) pkg. waffle-cut seasoned sweet potatoes

7 eggs

3 T. milk

Salt and black pepper to taste

½ lb. beef or pork chorizo, casings removed

2 T. canola oil

½ C. chopped onion

½ C. each diced red, yellow, and green bell peppers

1 tomato, chopped & seeded

8 (6") flour tortillas

5 bacon strips, cooked & crumbled

1½ C. shredded cheese

Salsa and chopped fresh cilantro, optional

Follow package directions to bake the sweet potatoes until crisp. Meanwhile, whisk together the eggs, milk, salt, and pepper; set everything aside.

In a large skillet over medium heat, brown the chorizo until crumbly and cooked through; drain and keep warm. Wipe out the skillet and heat oil on medium-high heat. Sauté onion for 3 minutes or until translucent. Add bell peppers and cook a few more minutes. Stir in the tomato and cook until warmed. Add set-aside egg mixture to skillet and cook with vegetables, stirring frequently, until eggs are done and everything is well mixed; keep warm.

Wrap tortillas in a damp paper towel and microwave about 30 seconds until warm and soft. Layer some sweet potatoes, egg mixture, chorizo, bacon, and cheese down the center of each tortilla and fold in half. Top with salsa and cilantro as desired. Serve promptly.

Makes 8

Spaghetti Tacos

In a large skillet, brown ½ lb. ground beef and ½ C. chopped onion until meat is fully cooked and crumbly. Stir in 1 (14 oz.) can diced tomatoes, 2 tsp. chili powder, and ½ tsp. each garlic powder, salt, and black pepper. Simmer until thick, 3 to 5 minutes, stirring occasionally. Meanwhile, cook 4 oz. spaghetti noodles following package directions; drain and toss with 1 tsp. olive oil. Add to the meat sauce and keep warm over low heat.

Preheat oven to 325°. Melt 1 T. butter and spread evenly over one side of 4 (7") flatbreads; sprinkle with garlic powder and grated Parmesan cheese to taste. Arrange flatbreads, cheese side up, on a rimmed baking sheet and cover tightly with foil; pop into the oven for 10 minutes or until warm and soft.

Gently fold each flatbread into a taco shell shape *(cheese side in)* and fill with spaghetti mixture. Sprinkle with shredded mozzarella cheese and fresh oregano or basil.

Twice-Baked Tacotatoes

Preheat oven to 375°. Scrub 4 large russet potatoes and pierce skins with a fork. Brush with vegetable oil and sprinkle with coarse salt. Wrap in foil if you'd like, or simply set potatoes on foil and bake for 1 hour or until tender. Remove from oven and reduce oven temperature to 350°.

When cool enough to handle, slice each potato in half lengthwise. Scoop out the pulp, leaving ¼"-thick shells. Place pulp in a mixing bowl and mash roughly. Add ¼ C. each butter and half & half, 3 T. taco seasoning, and salt and black pepper to taste. Beat on medium-high speed until fluffy, adding more half & half as needed. Spoon potato mixture into shells and sprinkle with shredded cheddar and Monterey Jack cheeses and cooked crumbled bacon. Bake on a cookie sheet 5 to 10 minutes to melt cheese. Top with green onions and serve with salsa and sour cream.

Makes 6

French Toast Wraps

2 C. vanilla yogurt

1 each banana and peach, peeled & sliced

2 eggs

½ C. milk

2 tsp. vanilla

1½ tsp. cinnamon

¾ tsp. ground nutmeg

6 (8") whole-grain or ultra-grain tortillas

Butter

2 to 3 T. cinnamon-sugar

1½ C. sliced fresh strawberries

½ C. fresh blueberries

⅓ C. granola cereal

In a medium bowl, stir together the yogurt, banana, and peach; set aside.

In a shallow bowl, whisk together eggs, milk, vanilla, cinnamon, and nutmeg. Dip both sides of one tortilla in egg mixture. In a skillet over medium-high heat, melt 1 teaspoon butter; add the tortilla and cook 1 to 2 minutes on each side or until golden brown. Sprinkle with some cinnamon-sugar and set aside. Repeat with remaining five tortillas, buttering the skillet each time.

Spoon some of the set-aside yogurt mixture down the center of each tortilla and sprinkle with a few strawberries and blueberries. Fold tortillas in thirds and top with more yogurt and fruit. Sprinkle with granola for a little crunch.

Impress brunch guests with this delicious wrap.

Salmon BLTs

In a small bowl, stir together 3 T. ranch dressing and 1 to 2 tsp. Sriracha sauce; set aside.

Preheat the broiler. Sprinkle 4 (4 oz.) salmon fillets with salt and black pepper and broil 4 to 5 minutes on each side or until pink and flaky. *(If you prefer, salmon may be grilled or baked instead.)* Remove salmon and keep warm. Turn off the broiler, but keep oven door closed so oven stays warm. Arrange 10 taco shells on a cookie sheet and place in the oven for 3 to 4 minutes to crisp up.

When ready to serve, flake the salmon. Load up each shell with some mixed greens, salmon, sliced cherry tomatoes, shredded cheddar cheese, diced avocado, and cooked crumbled bacon. Drizzle with the set-aside dressing mixture.

Taco Bowl Minis

Brown 1 lb. ground turkey in a large skillet over medium heat until cooked through and crumbly; drain. Stir in 2½ T. taco seasoning, ¼ C. water, and 1 or 2 seeded and diced jalapeños; cook until liquid is absorbed, stirring frequently. Reduce heat to low and keep warm.

Meanwhile, preheat oven to 350°. Arrange 30 mini fillo shells on a cookie sheet *(you'll need two 1.9 oz. packages)* and bake 3 to 5 minutes, until lightly browned and crisp. Fill shells with meat mixture and top with shredded cheddar cheese. Return to the oven for 1 to 2 minutes to melt cheese. Top with diced tomatoes and serve promptly.

Shredded Beef Fry Bread

1 lb. beef chuck roast

½ C. diced onion

2 cloves garlic

1 bay leaf

2 C. beef stock

½ tsp. each black pepper and dried oregano

1¼ tsp. paprika

2 tomatoes, diced

Salt to taste

8 pieces Homemade Fry Bread *(recipe follows)*

Shredded green cabbage

Toppings: shredded cheese, salsa, sour cream, and cilantro

Cut beef into 3" to 4" chunks. In a pot over medium-high heat, combine meat, onion, garlic, bay leaf, and stock; bring to a boil. Reduce heat, cover, and simmer 2 hours or until meat is very tender. Let stand until cool enough to handle. Remove beef, shred the meat, and set aside; reserve the stock.

In a dry pot, toast the pepper, oregano, and paprika over medium heat for 1 minute or until fragrant. Add shredded beef, tomatoes, and 1 cup reserved stock. Bring to a boil; reduce heat and simmer 10 minutes or until tomatoes fall apart. Season with salt and keep warm.

Prepare Homemade Fry Bread as directed. Top each piece with shredded beef *(drained)*, cabbage, and other toppings you like. *(We stirred taco seasoning into the sour cream for extra yumminess.)*

Homemade Fry Bread

In a large bowl, mix 3 C. flour, 1 T. baking powder, and 1 tsp. salt; stir in 1¼ C. warm water until dough forms. Knead lightly on a floured board to make soft moist dough that's no longer sticky. Shape into a 3"-wide log and cover with a towel for 10 minutes. Cut dough into 8 even pieces and roll into balls. With a floured rolling pin, flatten balls into 6" rounds, about ¼" thick. Fry in canola oil at 375° about 2 minutes per side, until golden brown and crisp; drain on paper towels.

Ice Cream Tacwiches

⅔ C. whole-wheat pastry flour

⅓ C. sugar

¼ tsp. salt

¼ C. milk

1 tsp. vanilla

2 T. butter, melted

2 egg whites at room temperature

½ C. dark chocolate chips

2 tsp. coconut oil

Ice cream

Sprinkles or chopped peanuts

Prop up several 1"-thick books like tents *(spines up)* and cover spines with waxed paper.

In one bowl, combine flour, sugar, and salt. In another bowl, whisk milk, vanilla, butter, and egg whites for 2 minutes; add to flour mixture and mix until smooth. Heat a large skillet over medium heat and coat with cooking spray. Pour about 3 tablespoons batter into pan and quickly spread in a 5" circle. Cook 1 to 2 minutes, until set and lightly browned on the bottom. Flip and cook 1 minute more *(still soft enough to drape)*. Gently drape over book spine and press lightly to form a taco shell. Repeat with remaining batter. Cool 1 hour.

Fill each taco shell with a big slab or scoop of ice cream and press together lightly. Freeze 15 minutes. Microwave chocolate chips and coconut oil for 30 seconds; stir and repeat until smooth. Drizzle chocolate over frozen sandwiches and top with sprinkles or nuts. Freeze again until hardened, or wrap individually and store in the freezer for a week or two.

Makes 8

Makes 6-8

Grilled Steak Tacos

¼ C. olive oil

Juice of 1 lime

2 T. minced yellow onion

1 tsp. minced garlic

2 to 3 tsp. ground cumin

1 tsp. each salt, chili powder, and Mrs. Dash Southwest Chipotle Seasoning

½ tsp. black pepper

1 to 1¼ lbs. flat iron steak

Taco seasoning to taste

½ C. sour cream

6 to 8 (6") flour tortillas, warmed

Prepared guacamole *(we used Wholly Guacamole)*

Pico de Gallo *(recipe on page 63)*

In large bowl, whisk together oil, lime juice, onion, garlic, cumin, salt, chili powder, Chipotle Seasoning, and black pepper. Add steak to the bowl and turn until well coated. Cover bowl and refrigerate 3 to 5 hours to marinate. Stir some taco seasoning into the sour cream and mix well; refrigerate for later use.

Preheat a grill to high heat. Place steak on an oiled grate and cook 2 to 3 minutes per side, brushing each side with marinade once *(discard leftover marinade)*. Reduce heat to medium and cook 15 minutes longer or to desired doneness. Remove from heat and let rest 5 minutes; slice into thin strips. Divide steak among tortillas and top with guacamole, Pico de Gallo, and reserved sour cream mixture.

Mexican Half-Moon Burgers

Preheat a grill to medium heat. Mix ½ lb. ground chicken, ½ lb. lean ground beef, 1 (4 oz.) can diced green chiles *(partially drained)*, and 2 tsp. chili powder in a bowl until well combined. Shape the mixture into four equal half-circle patties to fit inside a folded 6" flour tortilla *(straight edge at center)*. Grill the burgers on a foil-covered grate until almost done, flipping once. Season with salt and black pepper.

Place 4 (6") flour tortillas directly on the grate over indirect heat and set one burger on each tortilla, covering just half of it. Sprinkle each with ¼ C. shredded Colby-Jack, mozzarella, or Monterey Jack cheese. Close grill lid and cook until cheese is melted and tortillas are warm and have grill marks. Top burgers with guacamole, pickled jalapeños, lettuce, onions, salsa, and diced tomatoes as you like and fold tortillas over burgers like a bun. Olé!

Buffalo Chicken Bites

Preheat oven to 350°. Line a rimmed baking sheet with foil and spray with cooking spray; set aside. Wrap 10 (6") yellow or white corn tortillas in a damp paper towel and microwave 20 to 30 seconds to soften. With a 2½" to 3" round cookie cutter, cut two rounds from each tortilla to make 20 pieces. Set on prepped baking sheet and spritz tops with cooking spray; sprinkle with coarse salt. Bake 6 minutes; flip and bake 5 minutes more or until lightly browned and crisp. Let cool.

Meanwhile, in a saucepan over medium heat, combine ½ C. chicken wing hot sauce and 2 T. butter; stir and cook until butter melts. Stir in 2 C. finely shredded rotisserie chicken. Cook over low heat 5 to 10 minutes or until liquid is absorbed, stirring frequently. Top each shell with some chicken, sliced celery, sliced green onions, and blue cheese dressing. Sprinkle with blue cheese crumbles if you'd like.

Cream-Filled Cinnayums

1 C. heavy cream

Powdered sugar

¼ tsp. vanilla

1 (12.4 oz.) can refrigerated
cinnamon rolls

Canola oil for frying
(about 48 oz.)

2 fresh peaches

Fruit Fresh and water
(or lemon juice)

1 C. fresh blueberries

Zest of 1 lime, optional

In a chilled mixing bowl with chilled beaters, beat cream and 2 tablespoons powdered sugar until firm peaks form. Whisk in the vanilla; cover and refrigerate.

Separate the cinnamon rolls and reserve the icing for later use. Dust a cutting board generously with powdered sugar; coat both sides of each roll with more powdered sugar and flatten with a rolling pin to make eight 4" to 5" rounds.

Heat oil in a deep-fryer or deep skillet to 375°. Cook one round at a time until golden brown, about 1 minute per side. Drain on paper towels and carefully bend in half while very warm. Let cool completely.

Peel, pit, and chop the peaches. To prevent browning, dip in Fruit Fresh mixed with water as directed on package (or use lemon juice); drain well. Spoon set-aside whipped cream into shells and top with peaches, blueberries, reserved icing and/or zest before serving.

Fruit knows no limits—use whatever is in season and makes your taste buds happy.

Makes 8

makes 12-16

Spring Roll Mini Cups

¾ C. chopped grape tomatoes

¼ C. each chopped fresh cilantro and diced red onion

½ jalapeño pepper, seeded & diced

Juice of 1 lime

Pinch of salt

1 lb. lean ground beef

1 (1 oz.) pkg. taco seasoning (¼ C.)

⅔ C. water

1 (4 oz.) can diced green chiles, drained

1 pkg. spring roll or wonton wrappers

½ C. each shredded cheddar and Monterey Jack cheeses

Mix the tomatoes, cilantro, onion, jalapeño, lime juice, and salt in a bowl and set aside.

Preheat the oven to 350°. In a skillet over medium heat, brown the ground beef until crumbly and cooked through; drain. Stir in the taco seasoning and water; reduce heat to low and simmer until liquid is absorbed. Stir in the chiles and heat through; keep warm.

Meanwhile, spray a standard muffin pan with cooking spray. If using spring rolls, cut each wrapper into fourths or use whole wonton wrappers. Line muffin cups with one or two wrappers, creasing as needed to fit. Fill with beef mixture and top evenly with cheeses. Bake 8 to 10 minutes, until shells are lightly browned and crisp. Spoon some of the set-aside tomato mixture over each cup and serve promptly.

Twice as Nice

In a large skillet over medium heat, brown 1 lb. lean ground beef until crumbly and cooked through; drain. Stir in 1 (1 oz.) pkg. taco seasoning *(¼ C.)* and ⅔ C. water; bring to a boil, reduce heat, and simmer until thickened and most of the liquid is absorbed. Keep warm.

Meanwhile, spread ¼ C. refried beans over one side of each of 4 soft flatbreads. Place two at a time on a microwaveable plate and microwave 30 to 40 seconds or until warmed. Immediately wrap each flatbread around a crisp taco shell, pressing gently so bean layer sticks to shells. Fill with warm meat mixture and top with shredded cheese and lettuce, chopped tomatoes, diced onion, taco sauce, sour cream, black olives, or other favorite toppings.

Shrimpy Tacos

Preheat oven to 375°. Line a large cookie sheet with foil and spritz with cooking spray. Stir together ½ tsp. salt, 1 tsp. lime zest, and 2 tsp. chili powder. Sprinkle seasoning mixture over 24 large raw shrimp *(shells and tails removed)* and then transfer shrimp to prepped cookie sheet. Spritz with cooking spray and bake 5 to 8 minutes or until shrimp turn pink and are done.

Meanwhile, combine 1 peeled diced avocado, 1 T. lime juice, and ½ tsp. salt in a small bowl. In another bowl, stir together ⅔ C. sour cream and 1 T. minced chipotle peppers in adobo sauce. In each of 24 tortilla chip scoops, layer a spoonful of sour cream mixture, a few pieces of avocado, and one cooked shrimp. Sprinkle with fresh cilantro and more lime zest if you'd like.

Stuffed Zucchini Boats

3 medium zucchini

⅓ C. salsa

1 T. olive oil

1 tsp. each minced garlic, dried oregano, and smoked paprika

2 tsp. each chili powder and ground cumin

1 T. onion powder

½ tsp. cayenne pepper

1 (8 oz.) pkg. tempeh, crumbled

½ C. corn kernels (*fresh, grilled, or frozen & thawed*)

2 jalapeño peppers, seeded & diced

1 tomato, diced

¼ C. vegetable broth

¾ C. shredded Monterey Jack cheese, divided

Salt and black pepper to taste

Crumbled tortilla chips

Preheat the oven to 400°. Slice each zucchini in half lengthwise and scoop out the insides, leaving a ¼"-thick shell. Chop removed pulp and reserve ¾ cup; discard remainder. Spread salsa in a 9 x 13" baking dish; set aside.

Heat oil in a large skillet over medium-high heat. Stir in garlic, oregano, paprika, chili powder, cumin, onion powder, and cayenne pepper; cook 1 minute. Add the tempeh, corn, and jalapeños; cook and stir 3 minutes. Stir in tomato, chopped zucchini, and broth; cook until liquid is absorbed. Stir in ½ cup cheese and season with salt and black pepper. Divide tempeh mixture among zucchini shells and sprinkle with remaining ¼ cup cheese. Set upright in prepared dish and cover with sprayed foil. Bake 30 minutes or until zucchini is tender. Sprinkle with chips before serving.

Serves 6

Bacon, Eggs & 'Taters

6 bacon strips

4 C. cubed potatoes

3 T. taco seasoning

8 eggs, beaten

Salt and black pepper
  to taste

12 (6") extra thin
  corn tortillas

¾ C. shredded Monterey
  Jack cheese

Grilled Spicy Salsa
(recipe follows)

Preheat the oven to 375°. Cook bacon in a large skillet over medium heat until crisp. Drain on paper towels and crumble coarsely; set aside. Reserve 2 tablespoons bacon drippings in skillet and discard remainder.

Precook potatoes in the microwave about 3 minutes. Transfer to the skillet with bacon drippings and stir to coat. Sprinkle with taco seasoning and mix well. Cook 10 to 12 minutes over medium heat or until tender inside, stirring frequently. Set aside.

Cook and scramble the eggs in a sprayed nonstick skillet over medium heat until done. Season with salt and pepper and remove from heat.

Wrap tortillas in damp paper towels and microwave for 20 to 30 seconds to soften. Arrange tortillas in an ungreased 9 x 13" baking pan, bending in half gently next to each other to form taco shells. Fill each shell with about ¼ cup potatoes and some scrambled eggs and set-aside bacon. Top with cheese and bake 10 minutes. Serve with Grilled Spicy Salsa or another favorite salsa.

Grilled Spicy Salsa

Cut 1 tomato into ½"-thick slices and 1 onion into ¾" slices. Grill on a grill pan over medium-low heat until tender and caramelized, turning several times. Transfer to a blender and add 5 chopped garlic cloves, 2 chipotle peppers in adobo sauce, 2 T. lime juice, and 1 T. olive oil. Blend well.

Taco Salad Wraps

In a medium skillet over medium heat, brown ½ lb. lean ground beef or turkey until crumbly and cooked through; drain. Stir in ⅔ C. salsa, ½ C. canned chili beans *(with sauce)*, 1 T. Worcestershire sauce, 2 tsp. chili powder, 1 tsp. onion powder, ¼ tsp. garlic powder, and black pepper to taste. Bring mixture to a boil, then reduce heat and simmer uncovered about 5 minutes. Divide meat mixture evenly among 4 warm (10") flour tortillas and layer generously with shredded lettuce and diced tomato. Sprinkle with shredded Colby-Jack cheese, some salsa, and a few broken tortilla chips. Roll up burrito-style to enclose fillings.

Walking Enchilada Tacos

In a very large skillet over medium heat, brown 1 lb. lean ground beef until crumbly and cooked through; drain. Stir in all three packets from 1 (7.5 oz.) box Cheesy Enchilada Hamburger Helper *(the sauce mix, uncooked rice, and topping mix)* plus 1 C. milk and 2 C. hot water. Bring mixture to a boil. Reduce heat, cover, and simmer about 20 minutes or until rice is tender and most of the liquid is absorbed, stirring occasionally.

Remove from heat. Cut open 10 (1 oz.) snack-size bags nacho cheese tortilla chips. Spoon about ⅓ C. beef mixture into each bag and top with shredded Mexican cheese, lettuce, chopped tomatoes, salsa, and black olives.

Makes 8

Caramel Apple Pies

8 (6") flour tortillas

Canola oil for frying
  (about 40 oz.)

⅔ C. cinnamon-sugar

3 Granny Smith, Jonathan,
  or Jonagold apples

1 tsp. lemon juice

1½ T. butter

3 T. brown sugar

1 tsp. cinnamon

½ C. water, divided

1 T. cornstarch

Whipped topping

Caramel sauce

With a 4½" to 5" round cookie cutter or lid, cut eight circles from the tortillas. Heat 1½" oil to 375° in a heavy saucepan over medium heat. With tongs, place one circle at a time in the oil for 5 seconds; flip it over, fold in half, and hold in place 10 seconds until lightly browned. Turn and fry the other side until crunchy. Remove from oil and drain briefly on paper towels; coat with cinnamon-sugar. Let cool *(these may be stored at room temperature for up to 3 days)*.

Peel, core, and dice the apples; put them in a saucepan and toss with lemon juice. Add butter, brown sugar, cinnamon, and ¼ cup water; cook over medium heat for 4 minutes, stirring frequently. Combine cornstarch and remaining ¼ cup water; stir into pan and continue to cook until apples are soft and mixture is thickened, 15 to 20 minutes.

Divide apple filling among sugared taco shells. Add whipped topping and caramel sauce before serving.

Oriental Tuna Starters

18 wonton wrappers

Vegetable oil

¼ C. low-sodium soy sauce

1½ tsp. toasted sesame oil

2 tsp. Sriracha sauce

1 T. rice vinegar

Juice of 1 lime

1 tsp. sugar

2 tsp. grated gingerroot

1 or 2 (5 oz.) cans solid white albacore tuna in water, drained

1 ripe mango, peeled & diced

1 firm ripe avocado, peeled & diced

1 jalapeño pepper, seeded & diced

¼ C. diced red onion

1 C. chopped celery

1 T. snipped chives, plus more for sprinkling

1 tsp. sesame seed

Preheat the oven to 350°. Brush one side of each wonton wrapper with vegetable oil and place oiled side down on an inverted muffin pan, nestling each wrapper between two cups to make taco shells *(you can make six shells on one 12-cup pan)*. Bake 5 to 7 minutes or until lightly browned and crisp. Let cool.

In a small bowl, whisk together the soy sauce, sesame oil, Sriracha, vinegar, lime juice, sugar, and gingerroot; set aside.

Break up the tuna and combine with the mango, avocado, jalapeño, onion, celery, 1 tablespoon chives, and sesame seed in a large bowl. Drizzle with the soy sauce mixture and toss lightly. Let marinate about 10 minutes. With a slotted spoon, fill each wonton shell with some of the tuna mixture and sprinkle with more chives.

Try using thin pieces of sushi-grade tuna in place of canned tuna for a different twist on tacos.

Shortcut

No time to make the homemade wonton shells? Simply spoon the tuna mixture into tortilla chip scoops instead and get your party started.

Potato Olé Crisps

Preheat oven to 400°. Slice 3 medium baking potatoes into rounds, ⅜" to ½" thick; drizzle with 1 T. vegetable oil and toss to coat. Place in a single layer on a parchment paper-lined rimmed baking sheet. Sprinkle with coarse salt, black pepper, and Pinch Perfect Mexican Seasoning to taste. Bake 25 to 30 minutes or until tender and lightly browned, turning once halfway through cooking time. Let cool slightly.

Meanwhile, using a food processor, process 1 C. chopped walnuts, 2 T. vegetable oil, 2 tsp. chili powder, and 1 tsp. each ground cumin and smoked paprika until mixture looks like bread crumbs. Sprinkle warm potato slices with shredded cheese and top with sour cream, salsa, walnut mixture, and green onions. Serve warm.

Quickie Taco S'mores

Preheat oven to 375°. Toast 1 round frozen waffle until warmed through, but not crisp. Spread one side with creamy peanut butter followed by a layer of Nutella or chocolate frosting. Sprinkle with mini marshmallows. Gently fold waffle in half like a taco shell and tuck in a few segments of a milk chocolate candy bar. Sprinkle with chopped pecans. Set taco on a piece of foil and fold up the edges all around to form a "nest" to hold it upright; leave top of taco uncovered. Bake 4 to 6 minutes or until marshmallows puff up and begin to brown and shell gets slightly crisp. Repeat to make as many as you want. No campfire needed.

Puffy Chicken Tacos

1 (14.5 oz.) can salsa-style fire roasted diced tomatoes

⅓ C. chunky salsa

2 T. taco sauce, plus more for serving

8 bone-in chicken thighs, skin & fat removed

1 T. chili powder

2 tsp. each garlic powder and ground cumin

½ tsp. salt

1 C. uncooked instant white rice

Canola oil for frying *(about 48 oz.)*

2 (16.3 oz.) tubes Grands refrigerated biscuits

2 C. corn kernels *(grilled or canned)*

Toppings: lettuce, grape tomatoes, shredded cheese, and sour cream

In a large slow-cooker, combine the diced tomatoes, salsa, and 2 tablespoons taco sauce. Arrange chicken on top. Mix chili powder, garlic powder, cumin, and salt; sprinkle evenly over meat. Cover and cook on high 3 to 4 hours *(or on low for 6 to 8 hours)* or until done. Remove chicken and shred the meat, discarding bones. Return shredded chicken to slow cooker and stir in rice. Cover and cook on high about 1 hour longer.

Meanwhile, in a deep-fryer or heavy saucepan, heat 2" of oil to 375°. Separate the biscuits and flatten into thin 5" to 6" disks with a rolling pin. One at a time, fry dough in hot oil, about 1 minute per side, until golden brown and puffy. Drain briefly on paper towels and gently bend in half to form shells; keep warm. Fill shells with meat, corn, and the other toppings you like. Delish!

Makes 16

Greek Fish Tacos

Cucumber-Dill Sauce
  (recipe follows)

1 lb. firm white fish
  (such as tilapia or cod)

Salt and black pepper
  to taste

1 T. olive oil

8 (6") yellow or
  white corn tortillas

2 C. shredded green
  or red cabbage

1 C. sliced cherry
  tomatoes

¾ C. sliced Kalamata
  olives

1 cucumber, seeded
  & diced

½ C. crumbled
  feta cheese

Prepare the Cucumber-Dill Sauce as directed and refrigerate until needed.

Sprinkle both sides of fish with salt and pepper. Heat the oil in a large skillet over medium heat and cook fish 4 to 5 minutes on each side or until flaky and opaque. Remove from heat and flake the fish into bite-size pieces; keep warm.

Spray a clean skillet with cooking spray and heat each tortilla briefly on both sides to soften; keep warm. On each tortilla, layer some cabbage, fish, tomatoes, olives, and cucumber. Top with a little cheese and Cucumber-Dill Sauce to taste. Fold in half like a taco or serve flat.

Serve these tacos with lemon wedges for a perfectly zesty finish.

Cucumber-Dill Sauce

Peel and dice ½ English cucumber; place in a colander and sprinkle with 1½ tsp. salt. Set a plate on top and let drain 30 minutes. Pat dry and transfer to a blender. Add ½ tsp. minced garlic, 2 tsp. chopped fresh dill, and black pepper to taste; blend thoroughly. Pour into a bowl and stir in 2 (6 oz.) cartons plain Greek yogurt. Chill at least 2 hours before serving.

Makes 16

Cinn-ful Cheesecake Roll-Ups

1 lb. fresh strawberries,
  hulled & sliced

¼ C. water

1¼ C. sugar, divided

2 T. strawberry jam

1 tsp. cinnamon

2 (8 oz.) pkgs. cream
  cheese, softened

1½ tsp. vanilla

16 (6") flour tortillas

2 C. fresh blueberries,
  optional

Canola oil for frying
  (about 32 oz.)

½ C. butter, melted

In a saucepan over medium-low heat, bring strawberries, water, and ¼ cup sugar to a simmer and cook about 10 minutes. Mash berries and whisk in jam; simmer 5 to 7 minutes more, until thickened. Let sauce cool. Mix ½ cup sugar and cinnamon; reserve for later use.

In a large mixing bowl, beat cream cheese, remaining ½ cup sugar, and vanilla until smooth and creamy. Spread about 2 tablespoons cheese mixture over the center of each tortilla, leaving 1" around edges uncovered. Add some blueberries if you'd like. Roll up burrito-style, tucking in ends to enclose filling. Set seam side down and press lightly to hold.

Heat 1" of oil to 360° in a large skillet over medium heat. Fry filled tortillas about 45 seconds on each side or until golden brown, but still tender. Drain on paper towels. Brush butter over roll-ups and sprinkle with reserved cinnamon-sugar; let cool. Serve with prepared strawberry sauce.

Jerked Cod Boats

8 crisp taco boats
(see page 62)

1 T. each chopped fresh
thyme, chives, and
parsley

¼ to ½ tsp. red pepper
flakes

1 tsp. ground cumin,
grated gingerroot, and
minced garlic

½ tsp. each black pepper
and allspice

⅛ tsp. ground nutmeg

2 tsp. honey

Jicama Slaw
(recipe follows)

1 C. flour, plus more
for dredging

2 T. baking powder

1 tsp. salt

½ C. milk, plus more
for thinning

½ C. water

3 T. mayonnaise

Canola oil for frying
(about 48 oz.)

1 lb. cod, cut into fingers

Bake taco boats as directed *(or purchase crisp shells);* set aside. In a small bowl, mix thyme, chives, parsley, pepper flakes, cumin, gingerroot, garlic, pepper, allspice, nutmeg, and honey to make the jerk seasoning and use it to prepare the Jicama Slaw as directed.

In a medium bowl, mix 1 cup flour, baking powder, salt, ½ cup milk, water, and 1 to 2 teaspoons of remaining jerk seasoning to make a smooth thick batter; let rest a few minutes. Meanwhile, thin the mayonnaise with a little milk and set aside.

In a deep-fryer or heavy pot, heat 2" of oil to 375°. Working with a few pieces of fish at a time, dredge lightly in flour and coat in batter, shaking off excess. Fry fish until golden brown outside and white and flaky inside; keep warm. Fill warm taco boats with Jicama Slaw and fish; drizzle lightly with mayo mixture.

Jicama Slaw

Whisk together 1½ T. each honey and mayonnaise, 3 T. red wine vinegar, and 2 to 3 tsp. prepared jerk seasoning. Peel ¾ of a medium jicama. Julienne the jicama and 1 large Braeburn apple; add to honey mixture and mix well. Set aside to let flavors blend.

Mexicali Lettuce Wraps

8 large "cupped" lettuce leaves *(romaine, butter, or iceberg)*

2 ripe avocados

¼ C. fresh lime juice, divided

1½ C. chopped cherry tomatoes

1¼ C. chopped fresh cilantro, divided

3 T. olive oil, divided

Salt

2 tsp. minced garlic

2 T. canned diced green chiles

1 tsp. ground cumin

¼ tsp. cayenne pepper

1½ lbs. ground turkey

½ C. sliced green onions

Wash lettuce leaves and pat dry; set aside. Peel and dice the avocados and toss with 2 tablespoons lime juice. Stir in tomatoes, ¼ cup cilantro, 2 tablespoons oil, and salt to taste; cover and chill until serving time.

Heat remaining 1 tablespoon oil in a large skillet over medium-high heat. Sauté garlic and chiles about 1 minute; stir in cumin and cayenne pepper. Add the turkey and ½ teaspoon salt and cook until browned and crumbly. Stir in the onions and cook a couple minutes more. Remove from heat and stir in remaining 1 cup cilantro and remaining 2 tablespoons lime juice. Spoon some of the turkey mixture onto individual lettuce leaves and top with chilled avocado mixture. Wrap leaves around filling and serve promptly.

Makes 8

Grilled Veggie Tacos

Preheat a grill and grill pan on medium-high heat. Brush one side of 12 (10") flour tortillas with olive oil and lime juice; stack and wrap in damp paper towels. Set aside.

Cut 3 medium zucchini into ½"-thick slices and combine with 8 oz. baby Portobello mushrooms *(stems removed)*, 20 cherry tomatoes, and a little olive oil; toss well. Brush the outside of 2 bell peppers, 6 thick slices of red onion, and 3 ears of sweet corn with oil; set everything aside.

Lightly brown both sides of tortillas on the hot grill pan and fold in half to make shells; set aside. Transfer all vegetables to pan and sprinkle generously with taco seasoning, salt, and black pepper. Grill veggies until evenly browned, removing as they become tender. Place peppers in a bag, seal, and let rest 10 minutes; peel off the skins and thinly slice. Cut corn off cobs and coarsely chop all other veggies. Fill grilled shells with vegetables and drizzle with lime juice.

2-Bite Cookie Tacos

Wrap long 1" wood dowels *(or a broomstick)* with waxed paper and prop the ends between coffee mug handles to suspend dowels above countertop. Bake 1 (16 oz.) package preformed ready-to-bake refrigerated sugar or chocolate chip cookies as directed on package, slightly under-baking; cool on pans for 2 minutes. While still warm, remove cookies and drape over dowel to form shells. Cool completely before removing.

Beat together 1 (8 oz.) pkg. softened cream cheese, ¾ C. powdered sugar, and ½ tsp. vanilla on medium-high speed until smooth and fluffy; set aside. In a chilled mixing bowl with chilled beaters, beat ½ C. heavy cream until firm peaks form; add to cream cheese mixture and beat briefly to combine. Pipe filling into each shell. Add fresh fruit and sprinkles to sugar cookie shells; add M&Ms, chopped chocolate-caramel candies, and pecans to chocolate chip shells.

Serves 4

Cobb Salad To Go

2 T. each mayonnaise and buttermilk

¼ C. crumbled blue cheese

2 bacon strips

2 T. sliced green onions

1 tsp. minced garlic

2 T. red wine vinegar

1½ T. olive oil

¼ tsp. Dijon mustard

2 C. shredded rotisserie chicken *(or cubed ham)*

4 (8") whole-grain tortillas

2 C. shredded lettuce

½ C. diced tomato

1 ripe avocado, peeled & sliced

2 hard-cooked eggs, peeled & diced

In a small bowl, whisk together mayonnaise and buttermilk. Stir in cheese and refrigerate dressing until needed.

In a skillet over medium heat, cook the bacon until crisp; drain on paper towels and reserve drippings in skillet. Crumble the bacon and set aside. Add onions and garlic to the drippings in pan and cook about 1 minute, stirring often. Remove from heat; stir in vinegar, oil, and mustard. Add the chicken and toss to coat well. Keep warm.

Working with one at a time, briefly heat both sides of tortillas in a dry skillet over medium heat until warm and soft. Divide chicken mixture evenly among tortillas and top with some lettuce, tomato, avocado, eggs, and set-aside bacon. Drizzle with dressing. No forks needed!

Huevos Rancheros

Quick & Easy Salsa *(recipe follows)*

4 (6") corn tortillas or crisp tostadas

¾ C. shredded Mexican cheese

½ C. black beans, drained & rinsed

2 tsp. olive oil

4 eggs

Black pepper to taste

Sour cream

½ ripe avocado, peeled & diced

¼ C. chopped fresh cilantro

Lime wedges

Prepare Quick & Easy Salsa as directed. Preheat the broiler. If using soft tortillas, arrange them on a broiler pan and spritz with cooking spray. Broil for 2 minutes; flip and top each one with an equal portion of cheese and beans. Broil 1 minute more or until cheese melts. *(If using crisp tostadas, skip the cooking spray and first broiling and just top the tostadas with cheese and beans, then broil until cheese melts.)* Keep warm.

Heat oil in a large nonstick skillet over medium heat. Crack eggs into pan and cook about 2 minutes. Cover and cook 1 to 2 minutes longer, until whites are set. Set an egg in the center of each shell and season with pepper. Top with prepared salsa, sour cream, avocado, and cilantro. Serve with lime wedges.

Spray tortilla pieces with cooking spray; salt and bake at 400° until crisp, 6–10 minutes. Salsa-perfect!

Quick & Easy Salsa

Sauté ½ C. chopped onion in 1 T. olive oil in a large skillet until translucent. Add 1 (14.5 oz.) can fire-roasted diced tomatoes, ½ (4 oz.) can diced green chiles, 1 tsp. chili powder, 1 tsp. adobo sauce, and ½ tsp. ground cumin. Stir well, breaking up any large chunks, and simmer over low heat at least 10 minutes; keep warm. Tastes great with tortilla chips, too.

Pasta Shell Fiesta

12 uncooked jumbo pasta shells

2 T. butter

1 lb. lean ground beef

¼ C. each taco seasoning and water

4 oz. cream cheese, softened

1 C. diced tomatoes, divided

Black pepper to taste

¼ C. chopped fresh cilantro

2 green onions, chopped

¾ C. each shredded cheddar and Monterey Jack cheeses

½ C. crushed tortilla chips

Preheat the oven to 350°. Cook pasta shells as directed on package; drain. Toss with butter and set aside.

Meanwhile, in a large skillet over medium-high heat, brown the ground beef until crumbly and cooked through; drain. Stir in taco seasoning and water and cook until liquid is absorbed. Remove from heat and stir in cream cheese until blended. Then add ½ cup tomatoes and season with pepper.

Fill cooked shells with equal amounts of beef mixture and set upright in an ungreased 9 x 9" baking dish. Sprinkle with remaining ½ cup tomatoes, cilantro, onions, and both shredded cheeses. Bake uncovered for 15 minutes or until hot and melty. Sprinkle with chips and bake 5 minutes longer. Dig in!

Italian shells with Mexican fillings — the perfect mashup!

Serves 4

Waffled Cheese 'n' Chorizo

In a skillet over medium heat, brown 1 lb. pork chorizo *(casings removed)* until crumbly and cooked through; drain. In a microwavable bowl, stir together 1 C. canned black beans *(drained & rinsed)* and 1 T. each water and taco seasoning; microwave until warm. Set everything aside.

Preheat a waffle iron to medium high and spritz with cooking spray. Place 1 (6") flour tortilla on the iron and sprinkle with 2 to 3 T. shredded cheese *(try mozzarella, cheddar, or Colby-Jack)* and 2 to 3 T. cooked chorizo, leaving edges uncovered. Top with a second tortilla and press the lid closed firmly. Cook until cheese is melted and tortillas have brown waffle marks and are slightly crisp. Remove from iron and gently fold in half like a taco shell. Fill with some of the warm beans, sliced avocado, shredded lettuce, and Pico de Gallo *(recipe on page 63)*. Repeat to make five more.

Pumpkin Pie Rolls

Preheat oven to 350°. Coat 2 (7 x 11") baking pans with cooking spray and set aside. In a mixing bowl, beat together 1 (8 oz.) pkg. softened cream cheese and ½ C. sugar on medium speed until smooth and creamy. Add 1 (15 oz.) can pumpkin puree and 1 T. pumpkin pie spice; beat well and set aside.

In a small bowl, stir together ½ C. sugar and 2 tsp. pumpkin pie spice. In a microwaveable bowl, melt ¼ C. butter. Brush butter over one side of 8 (10") flour tortillas and sprinkle with sugar/spice mixture. Flip tortillas over and spread about ⅓ C. pumpkin filling over each, not quite to the edges. Roll up the tortillas and place them seam side down in prepped pans. Bake for 15 minutes. Cool in the pan about 20 minutes and then refrigerate. Serve cold with whipped cream, a sprinkle of cinnamon, and chopped pecans.

Makes 8-10

Lemon Cream Molasses Crisps

¼ C. each butter and
  molasses

2 T. each sugar and
  brown sugar

Scant ½ C. flour

¼ tsp. ground ginger

Pinch of salt

1½ tsp. vanilla

1½ C. heavy cream

¼ C. powdered sugar,
  or more to taste

1½ tsp. lemon extract

Sliced fresh strawberries

Zest of 1 lemon

Preheat the oven to 350°. Line two cookie sheets with parchment paper and set aside. Wrap long 1" wood dowels *(or a broomstick)* with waxed paper and prop the ends between coffee mug handles to suspend dowels above countertop.

In a saucepan over medium heat, combine butter, molasses, sugar, and brown sugar; stir constantly and simmer for 30 seconds. Remove from heat and stir in flour, ginger, and salt until smooth. Stir in vanilla. Working in small batches, drop batter by tablespoonful onto prepped cookie sheet, leaving 4" between cookies. Bake about 10 minutes or until cookies are flat, bubbling, and lacy. Remove from oven and let cool on pan 2 minutes or until cookies can be easily lifted off pan without wrinkling. Immediately drape each warm cookie over a dowel and let cool completely before removing *(shells should get crisp)*. Repeat with remaining batter.

In a chilled mixing bowl with chilled beaters, beat cream and powdered sugar until firm peaks form. Stir in lemon extract. Pipe whipped cream into each shell and top with berries and zest. Serve immediately.

Pork Carnita Salads

1 T. each salt and dried oregano

1 tsp. black pepper

2 tsp. ground cumin

2 T. olive oil, divided

1 (3½ to 4 lb.) bone-in pork shoulder roast, fat trimmed

1 C. coarsely chopped onion

1 or 2 jalapeño peppers, seeded & chopped

2 tsp. minced garlic

Juice of 2 oranges

Pineapple Salsa *(recipe follows)*

8 crispy taco bowls *(see page 62)*

Shredded lettuce

In a small bowl, stir together salt, oregano, pepper, cumin, and 1 tablespoon oil; rub the mixture all over the pork. Set meat in a slow cooker and sprinkle with onion, jalapeño, and garlic; pour in the orange juice. Cover and cook on low 8 to 10 hours *(or on high about 5 hours)*, until meat is very tender and falls off the bone. Meanwhile, prepare Pineapple Salsa as directed and refrigerate until needed. Bake taco bowls as directed *(or purchase them); set aside.*

Remove meat to a cutting board and shred when cool enough to handle, discarding fat and bone. Reserve juices, skimming off the fat.

Heat remaining 1 tablespoon oil in a skillet over medium-high heat and add shredded pork; press and cook until golden brown, flipping once. Add some reserved juices to moisten meat as needed. Fill taco bowls with shredded lettuce and top with some meat and prepared Pineapple Salsa.

Pineapple Salsa

Stir together 1½ C. chopped fresh pineapple, ¾ C. each diced red bell pepper and chopped red onion, 3 T. chopped fresh cilantro, 1½ chopped jalapeño peppers *(seeds removed)*, ¾ tsp. salt, 1½ T. lime juice, and 1 to 2 tsp. rice vinegar. Cover and chill.

Homemade Goodness

Crispy Taco Bowls

Press any size soft tortillas *(flour, whole grain, or flavored)* into purchased 6½" round nonstick tortilla pans to create wavy bowls. Bake according to package directions until lightly browned and crisp. Cool before removing and then fill with your favorite ingredients.

Crisp Taco Boats

Wrap 8 (6") corn tortillas in a damp paper towel and microwave until soft, 30 to 40 seconds. Spritz both sides of tortillas with cooking spray and sprinkle one side with coarse salt. Drape over two rungs of an oven rack and bake at 375° for 5 to 7 minutes or until lightly browned and crisp. Remove with tongs and let cool. These will hold a boat-load of yummy fillings.

Bulk Taco Seasoning

Stir together 5 T. chili powder, 2½ T. ground cumin, 2½ tsp. paprika, 2 tsp. salt, 1½ tsp. black pepper, 1¼ tsp. each garlic powder and onion powder, 1 tsp. each ground oregano and cayenne pepper *(or less to taste)*, and ½ tsp. ground coriander. Store in an airtight container. Use 2 to 3 T. of this mix to replace 1 (1 oz.) pkg. purchased taco seasoning. **Makes ¾ cup**

Pico de Gallo

Stir together 1 large diced tomato, ¾ C. finely chopped white or red onion, ½ seeded and diced jalapeño, 2 sprigs chopped fresh cilantro, 1 chopped green onion, ½ tsp. garlic powder, 1 to 2 T. fresh lime juice, and salt and black pepper to taste. Cover and chill at least 30 minutes. A delicious topping for any savory taco. **Makes 2 cups**

Index